What Time is it?

Edwin Kim

Ilustrated by
Mayara Nogueira

COPYRIGHT © ASCEND DIGITAL LLC
ALL RIGHTS RESERVED

Ready to start telling time? Practice reading clocks and get ready to sharpen your time reading skills. This book will teach you both hour and half-hour time format.

Dive into this wonderful and beautifully illustrated book as you begin this time telling adventure!

What time is it?

What time is it?

What time is it?

What time is it?

What time is it?

What time is it?

What time is it?

What time is it?

IT'S 1 O'CLOCK

one o'clock

What time is it?

What time is it?

IT'S 11 O'CLOCK
eleven o'clock

What time is it?

What time is it?

IT'S 5 O'CLOCK
five o'clock

What time is it?

What time is it?

What time is it?

What time is it?

What time is it?

IT'S 12:30
twelve-thirty

What time is it?

What time is it?

What time is it?

What time is it?

Author
Edwin Kim
edwinkim.co

Edwin Kim is a creative entrepreneur who loves to create inspirational books that can bring valuable lessons to the next generation. He happily creates stories and loves to bring his ideas to life.

Ilustrator
Mayara Nogueira
artstation.com/mayaranogueira

Mayara is passionate about the world of illustrated books. She loves drawing animals, historical and fantasy themes.

www.ingramcontent.com/pod-product-compliance
Lightning Source LLC
Chambersburg PA
CBHW040110120526
44589CB00041B/2992